TANDRA'S WORDS

Snapshots of Love, Faith and Mourning

—————————

TrUe ReAl

TrUe ReAl Books

TANDRA'S WORDS- SNAPSHOTS OF LOVE, FAITH AND MOURNING
Copyright © 2019 by True Real Books

ISBN 9781733885768

Printed in USA

I dedicate this to my wife, Tandra Rayner-Dye for teaching me how to be a better man, including putting my faith in God.

UNWRAPPING OURSELVES

The whispers of the rushing words that keep popping up when right is wrong and wrong is right.

As the sins of time become blameless through their eyes the fallen call out to their prayers for guidance.

But a legacy remains hungry for the life that cannot be afforded, the understanding of a child's hate for the world of love.

Our whispers to a world that needs to be unwrapped but time has no way around its indulgence, so we sleep with our sins.

Soon we rely on prayer!

TEAR DROPS

Our hearts didn't let the rebellion of what was to come stop the stolen moments called love, yet time has an angelic sense of humor.

It's as if the shattered pieces of glass written on parchment paper specifically speaks of a life through love and pain.

Yet we were to walk this path for so many years as one, but what I was missing was that you were actually healing me.

I believed that I was your true mission in life just when I thought you were mine.

Baby I waited in hopes that the mistake was just that a mistake that I would wake up from, but God slipped you away from this earthly world of dreams.

So I will blow a kiss to you every night in hopes that it reaches its eternal flame, the woman who would love this imperfect man.

SEEING YOU IN YOU!

When you peak inside the door but you've never left because you're inside the pain of death, your heart beats a little bit less.

Your encouragement slows down to a stop, yet the lights flicker on a hope that a breath overwhelms the stigma of its selfishness.

But your wants are lost in hate yet you remain, the pain sustains your detriment yet your eyes are open to a new world without order.

Stay blessed because Gods faith continues to control everything.

SPEAK TRUTH

Sometimes we have to look into our own souls praying
to open up the doors through our faith.

Yet, it's because we're so captivated in our own sins
that we lose touch with reality.

No one ever said an elegant peace would become a
stable choice for life, regardless of how much the
father would love you.

Perhaps it's like that black ink written on white paper
that hollers an un-coded truth, and just think we
won't see our final ending because it's actually the
start of the beginning.

A BOND

Just because we come into the world doesn't mean the world is of us, sometimes we can release ourselves.

So stop tripping because it hurts, and it's not fair, learn to love the grace that's given unto you.

Faith has a funny way of opening our eyes, and letting the spirit shine just a little bit longer, yet it causes us to watch and wait for a truth that will ultimately hurt, yet every breath relieves the soul.

I know my future even if it comes in such a short version, this is what life is to be so always remember I love you. I hope that you remember not the flesh but the spirit within!

ALPHA

This is when I was a child seeing through the glass eyes of a beautiful world made up of fragments.

When I spoke the word of my own prophecy I spoke them from my soul not knowing that they would be blessed before they were released. And at the same time my number would follow through the faith of my storms to come.

This is the time that I would learn that there's a inner peace that we never reach out for. We find ourselves glancing over it by asking ourselves why me, because in the beginning we do not know our true prophecy in life.

This is where the world becomes a cynical space and we're always in distress for healing.
But as students or healing has always been with us, it's called faith.

LIFE IS TRUTH

Lets make this more than fiction. A truth that will hit your heart, and make your soul fall in love.

I was wandering wounded through my hurt, praying for someone more than myself, but the tears didn't stay away.

I prayed my promise as my grandmother would say, he hears and sees the truth in your soul.

Being my grandmother's 1st born we had a special bond, my little hairless body ,but her little mini me.

As I grew we would have a love hate relationship, especially after finding out that I had a illness of the body.

And as ironic as it would be, I would fight the will of God but soon I would learn to obey, because God promised to be with me as he held me in his mercy, the ghost of the holy flowed through me lifting my spirits off the ground.

It was as if he was testing a child to grow into a saint, I understood what his love was truly about and the philosophy of the physical was over.

We are being tested for the greatest gift of all, life everlasting.

PROTECTING MY HOUSE

I knew that what he had for me was just for us, so I protected our house for you. I understood what you already knew, time would end.

I knew that you would not give up, that you would fight on so I protected you, and at the same time I spoke the truth to you.

I spoke of a time when I would not be here, that I accepted what my father had for me.

Baby the promise of love, faith, tears and your grace never went unnoticed even through our frustration we still loved.

I love the unconditional love we have for each other, you made me proud to be a mother, wife, and grandmother.

Our journey is not over. I'm just paving the way so follow your heart because your soul is already there.

My love is in your temple, the word is the way.

FAMILY LOVE

We have gifts that sometimes go unappreciated, like giving love to those who are sick.

Family should mean love for the body, and prayer for the soul.

Yet, we have an unloving relationship to speak God but play holy at the same time.

We forget!

I have seen True love through a real man of God who kept his word from the first day we met.

The words spoken from his heart, "I want to make love to you." Who would believe that my life would be so great because it was blessed to love him, but time still holds just a season.

So I remembered to plant my seeds into my husband's garden, so that he would remember our truth.

We can't love family from a far, then miss them in the spirit if we haven't been in their lives from the start.

LOVE

Love has no hesitation to hold me from writing our manuscript into the meaning of our life, or the ripples of the sea.

I love the calligraphy of your touch as my tears opened up to what my heart desires.

My cries to heaven's gate for more of you, yet with every beat of my heart I'm grateful for the Blessings bestowed on me, as I grow stronger in faith that love has blossomed.

The love that will never just be the touch of our flesh hypnotized in lust, I am your canvas so please open me up to the ends of our fate and the beginnings of our love.

So illustrate the ending as if it was the start of our beginning.

LIVING

To live knowing your deepest desires, last in the fear of leaving you behind to mourn what you would see again.

This was my protector in the body of evidence, the man who would grow in faith, yet would never give up on what was to happen.

I remember telling you that I understood my fate in the natural, that I would be with my father.

You see baby, as I ran through my grandmother's church I found out who I am, now my soul was at peace.

David, you held me as only a King could hold his Queen, but my love for my Father has sat me free.

I have no pain in the body of the present, no fear in the land of the lost. I am with him and I will wait for you.

Loving you.

25

SCARED

How can you be blessed with life within fear, scared of what is in front of you but hidden in the secrets of life?

Your heart is crying in crystal springs as the heavens capture your spirit yet your soul flows in peace.

No man has overcome his or her ignorance yet no one has faced there fears.

We deprive ourselves by being the selfish in this madness we call life, when we really don't know what life's about.

Memories of the truth as the heavens capture your spirit.

THE MESSAGE

Death comes in so many forms of unrealistic consequences, some can't be forgiven.

To be honest love is eternal, and unconditional yet a love one can call out the ultimate betrayal of glory.

When God gives you the power to speak life, it's expected that you will accept your hope for a better tomorrow.

We can't take back the disasters of following the enemy, just like we cannot say I'm sorry after the flesh is gone.

If you speak harm to the body of victory ,then you speak harm to yourself.

THIS EXISTENCE

In this world of chaos and sorrow we manage to give up so easily, our very existence trampled on our will to survive lost.

Sometimes we have a way out, but we just let it pass us by. You see we communicate with the Lord but we're too scared to follow his commands.

I remember when my heart echoed the same sentiment, yet God kept speaking to me, I am the way.

Sometimes we are lost, yet we find are way, even through the darkness that rises he shines the brightest.

Never quit, because he will never quit on you.

GIFTS

I lived my freedom knowing that God gave me my
dreams in such small pieces.

I loved my child.

You live to leave a legacy of life in the form of love
unconditionally, I raised a beautiful young man who
blessed me as a mother and grandmother.

I would say that my Father is outstanding and
phenomenal wouldn't you, I received all that I would
ever want in one man.

The man that God made just for me, mercy is
believing in the word and the word sat me free.

I love you, I love you.

MY PASTOR'S

To the body of the present, when the life needs the word to help in its transition to a higher plain.

I give thanks to my Pastors who saw love, and gave more in return. Pouring out the gospel of God into the flesh.

Helping me open my eyes, but must importantly saving our home.

I do understand that my husband will need you more now then ever, now that I'm gone, even if he says he's okay.

This is love at its simplest, yet ultimate glory.

I give thanks to the body of Christ for you who would bless me in life.

SISTERS

To my click, my sisterhood I will forever be grateful for the love that transformed me into what we would become, friends.

Your love for the person not the illness, blessed my soul to its core. It gave me the chance to walk the beaches with my prayer worries.

I still feel the sun.

I was given a true love that shined brighter than the sun, yet crashing deeper than the sands of time.

We will forever have stories of love and laughter, so smile with me because I am walking and waiting to flourish with you again.

True sisters for life.

YOUR HEART

Yes we knew what was to happen would come some
day, yet your heart wouldn't let go. I knew that.

Some grow old, but we grew stronger as one.

Your pride didn't let you want anything for yourself,
but everything for me, you wouldn't let go me.

Baby it's okay to cry because you loved this vessel,
and cherished my soul.

That's why I hope that writing these poems together
can help to heal you, and teach others that love is a
lifelong peace.

Your always my TrUe ReAl

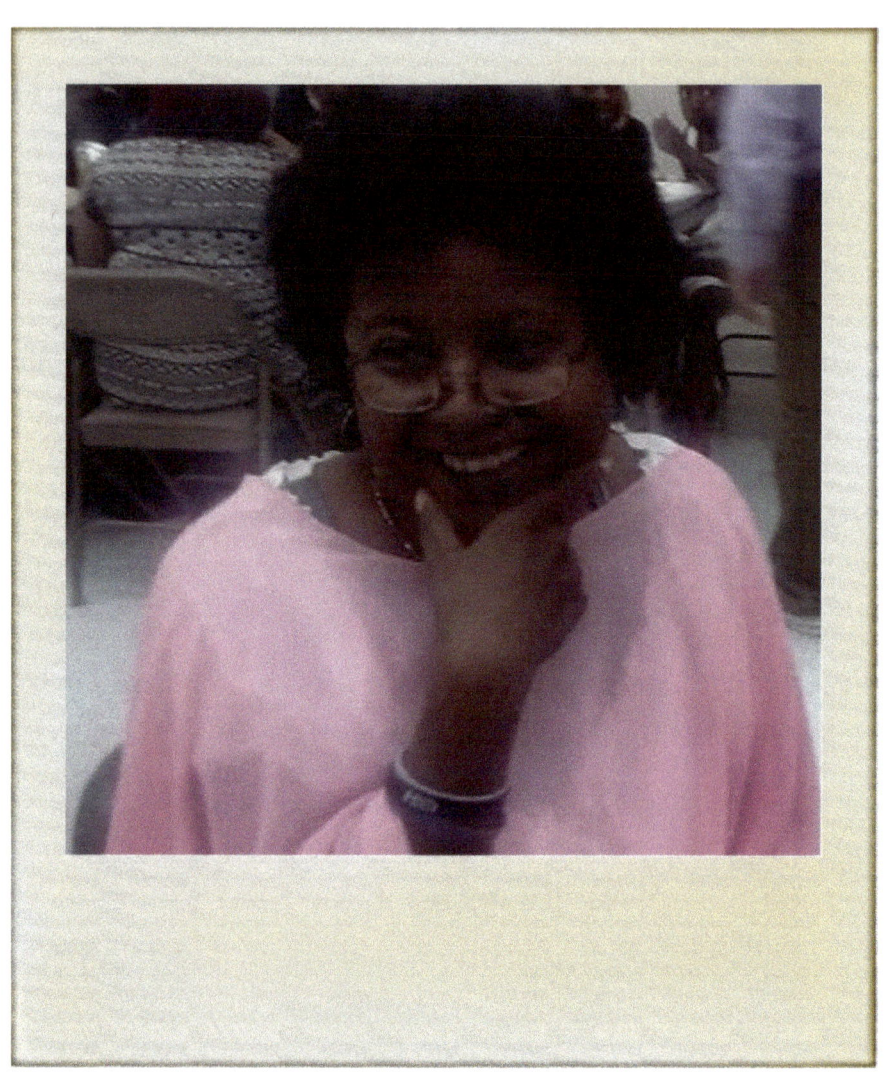

AMAZING ISN'T IT

We justify our existence as a people, but won't give
God our truth, perhaps we should change.

Luke warm cannot be a place we can afford, we only
ask for our gifts during the holidays.

My Lord, My God rains his Blessings through the
ultimate waste lands of the storm.

Blessed our we who chose hot over cold and never
except warm over him.

I am his child.

RELEASE

Remember that we are stacked against all odds of our memories, left to stand in his presence, touch me Lord.

Show me my road to travel even if comes with detours, let me not be derailed by the enemy within because your word holds true.

This vessel of a body may hurt, but you are still in me, God I Love You, because there is no other way and no other team I would rather be on.

You are my victory the battle is yours.

By His wounds
we are healed

Isaiah 53:5

MEDICINE FOR LIFE

When I received my diagnosis it came as a shock, not because of the diagnosis, but because of the time I had left to teach.

My canvas was a man who would go through so many challenges, yet still needed to heal.

My God only gives you what you can handle.

The message would be therapy for us to love not the body, but the spiritual boundaries that would open.

For some reason my job manifested itself through the hands that God placed in front of me.

Write with wisdom so that your heart show our sacrifice.

MY ROAD

Walking the path that we all one day will cross, is not easy.

You see.

I can't say that I'm not scared, because of what is to come, yet my God will lead me through.

I found that living has always been a test of trials and tribulations, all for a lifetime to be blessed.

We're not strong enough to survive alone if we don't give him the prays.

So if I can feel as if I made a difference from the lesson learned than I have grown in wisdom.

I am not afraid anymore.

DESPAIR

I saw what I believed was a broken plan trying to take me through this journey of the lost without him.

The what if's, and why me? I feel the blessings when you try to tell me it's going to be alright, that's only our love speaking.

Then on the other hand telling me that somebody else is going through the same thing, the God in you, always trying to make everything alright.

Your entrapment of trying to hold me through the rain, yet in the storm as if I'm trying to lose all hope.

I see bravery at its best, so I will continue to hold my hands to the heavens, as if I knew what he has instore for me.

I have been blessed with the belief that a new day is coming, a supernatural healing is coming because I will soon be with him.

Prayers for the lost.

MY DARLING

I excepted my challenges in life as you made sure that our life style never changed, the lord working through the body of the obedient.

My God kept the torch lights on during the hard times when we didn't understand our way.

Yet we followed him, sometimes being defiant but obedient all the way.

I have made my transition from the Earthly chains that bind us now it's up to you to complete our journey.

Teach others to respect the words that they deliver unto our Lord the day they say I do, that it binds them throughout all costs.

You are my last victory in the flesh and I give thanks to the God who brought our souls together.

David I love you.

I am the Lord who heals you.

Exodus 15:26

THE SPIRIT OF THE BODY

Baby I saw the pain that you tried to cover up just to make my life easier, when working for others has no loyalties to the family.

No one ever knew that you would come home on your breaks to clean and make sure that I was loved and cared for.

Like I would say, God is good because he gave me my dream in such a big package.

Our souls are forever intertwined so stay oblivious to the world of man and let your obedience in our Lord remain unwavering.

Beauty awaits you in the bosom of his love.

I will be there, love you.

WE ARE ONLY HUMAN

It's irrelevant right now how we forsake our love ones
as we're speaking our false faith.

Your family should be able to deposit their trust in
you, but we are only human, flesh subjected to the
world.

I learned that we should depend on God to guide our
steps that way we can recognize the importance
through our faith.

I can't say that I'm disappointed in the illustration of
mistrust because I am with the most High.

You can only soar with Him if you believe the Word.

MY TEACHER

Subscribe to the body of the glory that's in his presence, let the pain rejoice in him.

Give until you hear your heart reveal the truth that I am the true Jehovah.

So read and submerge your spirit into the Holy Ghost that creates eternal heavens so that I will light the stars.

Subscribe to the ultimate website via the truth.

I love you.

MY PROTECTOR

I found out that when your being attacked God shields us like a antivirus agent.

He constantly gives us details on how to rebuild and defeat the enemy, replacing him with the will of God.

We cannot afford to live without sorrow and pain if we are not tested in this world, because in grieving and hurt we become stronger through him.

You are the ultimate word because in growing in him we begin to stand the test of time.

His promises are kept if you just stand still.

NEVER ALONE

I found that standing on hallowed ground remains unknown in the presence of the body, yet we keep asking for what is already ours.

It's because at times we're never reaching for our spiritual guidance, yet we hope that without work it will be provided to us.

So we as a people continue to remain locked up in our own prisons, while sentencing ourselves remains our own doing.

Trust in the process and let God fulfill His promise

Trusting Him.

IN THE PRESENCE OF THE BODY

I'm feeling weak right now, but this body of a vessel, of a shell can't hold its food, yet my Father still feeds me. He alone provides comfort in the presence of what is already written.

Even though husband tries to cover up his tears, I am so lucky to have a man who served his God with faith.

My spirit is at peace knowing that even in pain he will rely on the most high to comfort him, I do love this man.

He will miss the kisses that brought us to this point. I know he will remain unwavering in the works that have to be done. I am with you in the spirit.

I fell in love with a real man of God.

ALL FOR YOU

Who wouldn't give everything to stand in the grace
and presence of our God.

To praise him through the storm and any other
situation that shall arrive.

So I praise my God because he takes the pain away, I
will stand still in his presence and be obedient to his
wishes.

So stand in your position and shout, wont he do it!

THE WAIT IS OVER

You're not alone in this world, you are being freed through your soul in the midst of your beginning, the journey is here.

Your are free from the shackled child who wasn't allowed to cry, it's time to find your strength in me, and in her memory. She awaits your arrival, but until then you have my work to carry out.

I have been the overseer from the beginning, and the ending from the start. I am the Alpha and Omega of your life.

Now it's time to do it my way, you are exactly where you need to be.

THIS HOUSE

We should give him a never ending praise when the body speaks his holy name, so when we bask in the glory of a outstanding love.

A love that's bursting to teach a eternal life through the word that ends in his mercy.

I find that we are only living through the sacrifices of his own understanding, to live in the sanctuary that is blessed.

Even though my days were not easy to bare, and my body turned on itself. I gave the pain and suffering to Him. I lived by his words that I will be saved.

He will never forget, nor forsake the truth of His child.

REFLECTION

I'm saying this for personal reasons, but believe me I am speaking directly to you Lord.

Father of a higher power we are nothing but skin, bones, and tissue without you. We carry such heavy burdens in our hearts, especially when it comes to losing someone whom we love so dearly.

The pressure of trying to hold on without saying goodbye, causes our emotions to take us through the agony of not wanting to let go.

But you are still there even when our anger is pointing at you, It's in this very moment our sanity is being held by a thread but you do not waiver in the mints of the truth.

That's the beauty of your love.

WORSHIPPERS PRAYER

With my love Lord, and multitude multiplied in me, has brought me to an understanding that my action will not be of me.

Oh God, Father, my Hallelujahs belongs to you. I am safe in the bosom of your glory, your heart adores me.

The King of all Kings, and it's in my destiny to meet you at the cross roads of destination, where peace is love.

Jesus, I release it in the atmosphere that you are perfecting the me.

SANCTUARY

We as the temple of flesh will never understand the hurt in us if we do not search out our fixer.

He is not the pain that you can rejoice in without a challenge.

But he is in the final battle that you shall win, because the pain is just a substitute that the enemy relies unto you; give in.

We should always understand that when you're in love with the most high, you are in love with it all.

There can only be one.

STAYING IN YOUR PLACE

Sometimes we want just a little bit to much and never enough from our Father, but faith based on nothing receives nothing.

I'm not sure how you will take this but please understand, we ask him to help us and because it doesn't come how we want it to turn out, we turn our backs on our Savior.

Jesus only said that it would be of his will and his way, remember what he himself had to endure for our sins.

So when the body hurts it's all for him, when your tired and think you cannot take anymore it's for him.

So when you thirst for knowledge It's all because of him.

You can't live in secret, when you love my God.

ENTERING THE KINGDOM

I'm figuring things out as I grow deeper into the works of the Lord, the body of his holy spirit.

The company of his flesh that ultimately holds the truth in him, that we have been given a key and a number.

The keys holds the answer to opening up the lock to our final sanctuary; our glory.

Yet the number holds our time left to do his work on this plan. We have choices to make or break and it's all up to you.

Do not miss out by running past your cycle.

FRIENDSHIPS

I found out what the true Jehovah was to me through the my friends who would help guide me closer to him.

They would show me that God was always and forever will be my protector and provider.

We find spiritual guidance through his word, but if we do not surround ourselves with those who are true believers, then we can make mistakes out of mistrust.

I was blessed at such a difficult time in my lifetime as fear tried to take over.

But my God allowed me to make a way with the help of my Earthly power squad.

Start putting your pieces together.

I HAVE BECOME

History of a love written before the world had
become, the blessings of God with faith.

There's nothing that I can't do to rain down my life
through the words of my justice provided by my
blood.

You have nothing but time and the pleasures of
eternity to live until you meet again.

I see the worldly side effects of a shell forfeited by the
hearts shattering pieces, the glory of the flesh.

I love you more than you would know.

HIDING IN HIS PRESENCE

If you hide how can we seek the glory, if you know the words how can you live across from them, we must put our loyalties in the truth of his presence, we should live how we want to walk in life without fear of being untruthful and ignorant to his will.

Our Pastor's hold the authority over our realty, but they too have a responsibility to be true to themselves, people make love, people have real problems and people soul should be there ultimate glory.

With a unwavering commitment to make sure that we loosen the chains that bind us from our inheritance.

You too have a soul that fights through its immortal problems.

MY SIGNATURE

I had to forge my way through my obsession with my psychological hearts desires in order to believe that he would keep his word to love me and provide sanctuary through his grace.

He showed me my new beginning, but I would have to give up my ending in order to hold onto the world of man.

I would have to springboard myself into my own prosperity that is of a Hebrews commandments to live by.

Wouldn't it be great if we gave up on making the physical world about us, and sign our own serenity to him who holds our true love.

Sign up for the greatest gift card you will ever need.

TESTIMONY

We generate a beautiful untruth when we do not
rejoice in the gathering of our faith, sleeping on him.

We cannot slip and slide on a true testimony if open
our eyes to God who provided the ultimate text book
to life.

As he laid down his glory resting on the cross for his
family to return to their rightful home.

The doors have opened as
blood drips through the body of the spiritual world,
he cleanses me.

Testing us to find out who he really is as well as who
we would ultimately become.

This isn't a test if you know the answer.

10%

Every day we give our time to a television watching the young become restless as we sleep on God.

We play with God as if we're riding off into the sunset, while keeping our pockets fat, but when it comes to giving ten percent to the most high, we fall short of his blessings.

We fake like something always comes up when it comes to giving God his.

In this way we put on our blindfold when it comes to our Lord what his blessings has done for us, but we are sanctimonious in what we ask for.

When we should freely give in order to show him our willingness to submit to is will.

Let the spirit lead you to him.

Water

I find myself inching forward towards the water's edge seeking my own testimony, looking for a way to survive.

Yet, the enemy tries to hold me down, trying to take my breath, for my love for the Lord through my fears.

I still hear you Father the ripples caring your voice, I'm holding onto your every word.

You are my victory Father, the ultimate Alpha and there is no other way but to follow grace in its ultimate form.

You are the perfect moment in my life, the waters of my future.

WEIGHING THE DIFFERENCE

When it comes to having just a little understanding of
what this one simple word means we lose our minds.

Do we really appreciate, or grasp the true real
meaning of praising the Lord Jehovah's name?

Let's take a moment to understand what the world
has intended for his people.

To be blinded and led astray, to be captured by
Immersing yourself in the enemy's false tells.

Forfeiting the knowledge that has been given to you.
We must mentally understand the overwhelming
choices that we have in life.

Because like the good book says "My people perish
for lack of knowledge".

I can only give you a number, but please know that
the truth is covered in my blood.

A LIFETIME

Divided by the clouds and wherever you see, I will be there to love you sweetheart.

God brought our hearts through our passion for the flesh to the love of our souls.

We are forever intertwined, connected to a tether lock together in a knot.

I am thankful for Jesus's unconditional love that came with no excuses for the beauty within you.

Thank you for listening to his will to grow stronger through him.

IF YOU COULD ONLY IMAGINE

If you could see what happens to the body after the soul returns to ashes to ashes.

A dusty shell forfeited by the weakness of not being able to focus on its true life in heaven.

In so many ways we are truly blessed by faith based on the spoken words of our God, yet we can be led astray by the sounds of pleasure.

We are just the vehicle stuck in slow motion, but the vessel of the body has to mentally grow into the temple of the word before it can learn.

What an unlimited Blessing this could be.

IN DARK PLACES

Sometimes we find ourselves in a dark place cold, and alone left with our own thoughts of despair.

That's when we should give everything unto him to bind and hold the spirit within the word.

Binding that new born child, as they suckle the milk of life, free flowing the spirit into its trilogy of the truth.

That's what he freely gives; life everlasting in his presence, so we must pray for a better understanding to live.

The early hours of the darkness come so we can speak our new language; speak to him.

ARE WE READY

There once was a time when a pastor would only ask are you ready when you were weathering your storm during your season.

It would free-up the freedom in you, unlocking that very part of your spirit and opening up your eyes to a new day.

Are you ready for your new birth-certificate of releasing God from the spiritual realm, the cleansing?

The baptism of the body is coming so I ask you again, are you ready for the greatest journey of them all?

The preacher of all Kings speaks.

BLOWN AWAY

We are truly like draft wood slowly blown away,
transitioning our lives with the wind, blossoming
through every stage of the storm.

Cracking through the clouds like lightening striking
the ground, pounding for more of him, praying and
surrendering it all.

Can't you see that we are finally living our truth,
blown from our mistakes as we except our
inheritance?

We now know what "walk by faith and not by sight"
truly means.

JUDGMENT

Do not cry for the beloved, rejoice for the grace that
has been bestowed unto me.

I am the tears flowing through the rain, and the
rainbow in the midst of the your storm.

Do not cry because the fruit is now yours to learn. Eat
of it, and grow within the wisdom of my Fathers love.

Do not let the hurt bind you in its cataclysm of pain,
stand still knowing that you have done my Father's
work, I am proud of you.

May the wisdom of his knowledge and love comfort
you in your time of resting, David I love you.

ACKNOWLEDGEMENTS

First and foremost I thank God for giving me the strength to write this book through my tears. To my aunts and uncles, and friends who have supported me through the ups and downs. A very special thank you, and gratitude to those friends and family for loving and taking care of my wife, by giving her hope and joy over the years.

Poetry, is my way of expressing my truth. It's like one's presence, if it doesn't make an impact, your absence will not make a difference.

Be Blessed.

TrUe ReAl
David Maurice Dye

CPSIA information can be obtained
at www.ICGtesting.com
Printed in the USA
LVHW051117150719
624096LV00010B/905/P